What do you do with a
GRUMPY
KANGAROO?

by Jane Belk Moncure
illustrated by Linda Hohag
and Lori Jacobson

GROLIER
B O O K S

Grolier Books is a division of
Grolier Enterprises, Inc.,
Danbury, CT.

Published by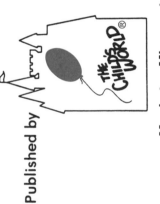

THE CHILD'S WORLD®

Mankato, Minnesota

The Library —
A Magic Castle

Come to the magic castle
When you are growing tall.
Rows upon rows of Word Windows
Line every single wall.
They reach up high,
As high as the sky,
And you want to open them all.
For every time you open one,
A new adventure has begun.

Tony opens a Word Window.

Guess what
Tony sees?

What do you
do with a
Grumpy
kangaroo?

A grumpy kangaroo. What can Tony do?

"I will try to help grumpy Kangaroo.
I will be his friend," says Tony.

He takes grumpy Kangaroo to

the circus and buys him a balloon.

They watch the elephants do tricks,

the ballerinas dance, the ponies prance . . .

the tumblers

tumble,

and the clowns make funny faces.

12

Guess what?

Grumpy Kangaroo begins to giggle.
He makes funny faces too. He is a
happy kangaroo, until . . . .

his balloon pops!

pop!

He begins to cry. Now he is a sad kangaroo. What can Tony do?

He buys sad Kangaroo
a new balloon.

Now Kangaroo is a glad kangaroo.

That is, until . . . .

he drops the string and the balloon

flies away. Now Kangaroo is a

mad kangaroo.

When Tony takes mad Kangaroo to the park,

guess what mad Kangaroo does?

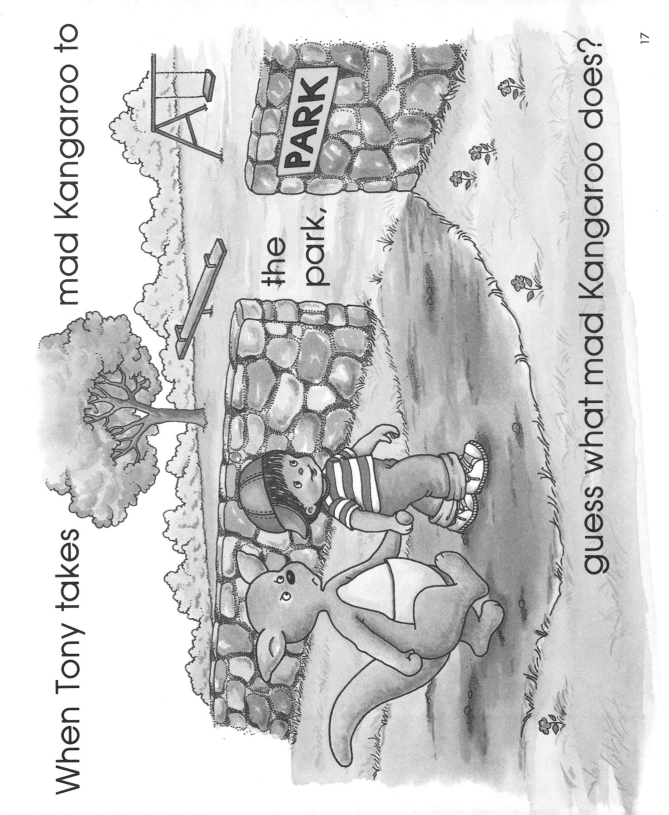

He bumps Tony on the see-saw.

Bump . . . bump.

"Bad Kangaroo," says Tony. So Kangaroo . . . .

says, "I'm sorry. I won't bump you anymore."

"Good Kangaroo," says Tony.

"Let's go down the slide."

When Kangaroo gets to
the top of the slide,
he is . . .

afraid
to go
down.

Kangaroo is a scared kangaroo, until
Tony goes down first.

Now Kangaroo is a
brave kangaroo.

Down
he goes . . . .

zoom!

Brave Kangaroo says, "Let's ride bikes."
Down the hill they go . . . zoom!

But Kangaroo goes too fast. He

tumbles off his bike.

Now Kangaroo is a hurt kangaroo.

What can Tony do?

He puts a bandage on Kangaroo's knee. Now Kangaroo is sleepy.

He is a sleepy,
fussy kangaroo,
so . . .

Tony puts him to bed for a nap.

When Kangaroo wakes up, he is a joyful, jumpy kangaroo.

"Let's jump rope," says Joyful, Jumpy Kangaroo. And they do.

Little Kangaroo keeps on jumping.
He jumps all the way home to the zoo.

And Tony closes the Word Window.

You can read these words with Tony.

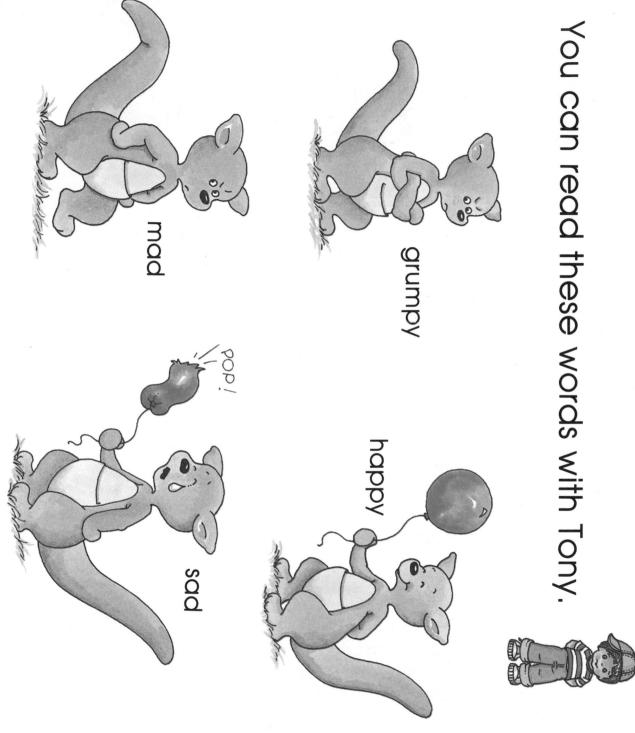

mad

grumpy

happy

sad

POP!